C000092016

Teresa of Avila

by
Jennifer Moorcroft

*All booklets are published thanks to the
generous support of the members of the
Catholic Truth Society*

CATHOLIC TRUTH SOCIETY
PUBLISHERS TO THE HOLY SEE

Contents

Early life

In 1920, a Jewish philosopher, Edith Stein, picked up a copy of the *Life* of a sixteenth century Spanish nun, Saint Teresa of Avila, while staying in the house of a Catholic friend. She stayed up all night reading it, and at the end she said, 'This is the truth.' Within a short while she had become a Catholic, and later entered the Discalced Carmelite Order that Teresa had founded. In 1942 she died in the gas chambers of Auschwitz.

Who was this nun, whose writings have had such a profound influence on generations of souls, especially those seeking a deeper life of prayer, and who in 1970 was declared a Doctor of the Church? As if presciently, it is said that King Philip II of Spain, Teresa's contemporary, had placed his copy of her *Life* between the works of Saint John Chrysostom and Saint Augustine, who were both Doctors of the Church.

Hers was a remarkable life. She was born in Avila on 28th March 1515, where her father, Alonso de Cepeda, was a wealthy merchant. Alonso's father, Teresa's grandfather, was a *converso*, a convert from Judaism, a stigma in those days that he was eager to put behind him. In Avila, he was able with the wealth he accrued to obliterate this shame, and with his wealth was able to buy a title that enabled him to affix 'Don' to his name. His son Alonso furthered the family's rise by marrying Catalina del Peso, a farmer's daughter with a pedigree. She died within two years of marriage after bearing him two children. After a decent period of mourning, Alonso married the fifteen year old Beatriz de Ahumada, who had the prized distinction of being from an 'Old Christian' family. The de Cepeda's place in honoured society was established.

Large family

Beatriz de Ahumada bore ten children, Teresa being the third child and the first daughter, the 'most beloved of them all'. Unsurprisingly, Beatriz spent a good bit of her time in bed, reading the latest novels and had a stock of religious reading. Girls were not given a formal education, apart from the household skills they would need later on in married life, but Teresa learned to read early, probably taught by her mother. To begin with, her favourite reading was the lives of the saints. Rodrigo, her favourite brother, was four years older and the two of them fed their imagination on the heroic deeds of the martyrs - and their heavenly reward eternal happiness - for ever and ever! This became their mantra - happiness, forever and ever. Ever practical, even at such an early age - she was seven at the time of her exploit - Teresa planned her strategy to gain such a wonderful reward as quickly as possible. The quickest way, she decided, was to have her head chopped off by the Moors, and so she and Rodrigo decided they would go and declare themselves Christians to obtain such a desirable outcome. With some raisins wrapped in a napkin for sustenance, they set off, but were barely beyond Avila's formidable walls when an uncle caught up with them and brought them back home.

Teresa then consoled herself with building hermitages in the spacious garden, which fell down as soon as they were constructed, and organising the other children in religious life - with herself as Prioress. However, Teresa was growing up into a most attractive twelve year old - and knew it - and her love of adventure was inclining more towards the tales of chivalry and romance that her mother loved. She was also influenced by some young and rather worldly cousins who came to their house. Her father disapproved of them, but could not very well forbid them coming, as they were relatives. Teresa loved perfume and jewellery, although she was always discerning.

Convent boarding school

In the midst of her burgeoning femininity, Teresa's mother died when she was thirteen years old, and Teresa turned to Our Lady as being her mother now. It did not stop her long from loving frivolous pursuits, and when a possible liaison between his young daughter and a cousin became the subject of covert gossip, Don Alonso decided that it would be better for her to be sent away from temptation. When she was sixteen, then, soon after her elder sister Marie had married and could no longer chaperone her, Teresa was sent to a nearby Augustinian convent boarding school.

Teresa said that she was quite pleased about the move because her lifestyle was beginning to bore her, and being so adaptable she soon settled into her new life. Some of her youthful fervour returned, yet she found prayer hard. She envied those girls who could dissolve into sentimental tears of devotion, but was too honest not to be true to herself. A nun at the convent, Doña Maria de Briceño, was a kind and sympathetic guide for her, and also a woman of deep prayer. She rekindled in Teresa a desire for prayer, but Teresa was not at all sure that she wanted to be a nun. Neither did she want to be married. She saw that it was a very restricted life, as married women never went out unescorted, and most of their life was spent within the four walls of their house. Paradoxically, nuns often had more freedom to move about outside their convents.

Vocation

After eighteen months at the convent, this struggle within her may well have contributed to a breakdown in her health. She suffered from fainting fits and high fever, so it was decided to send her away to recuperate with her sister Maria, who now lived in the countryside. To break the journey, she stopped for a few days at the house of her Uncle Pedro, a dry and religious recluse. Here she started reading religious books again, and came to a decision - a somewhat pragmatic one: 'I began to grasp the truth which I had heard as a child, that all is nothing, and that the world is vanity and on the verge of ending. And I began to be afraid that if I had died right then, I would have gone to hell. Even though I couldn't make myself want to become a nun, I saw that that was the best and safest thing to do; and so, little by little, I decided to bully myself into doing it' - to become a nun. Not through love of God but from fear of hell.

Her health did not improve at Maria's house, so Teresa returned home and started her campaign to win Don Alonzo's consent to her entering a convent. Her father wanted his very personable daughter to make a good match and enhance his own social status, but Teresa was adamant that she would never marry. She had decided she would enter the Convent of the Incarnation, just outside the walls of Avila, where Juana Suárez, a friend of hers, was already a nun.

Since her father was adamant in his refusal, Teresa took matters into her own hands. Accompanied by her brother Antonio, during the night of 2nd November 1536, she slipped out of the house and made her way to the Convent of the Incarnation. It was not an easy decision.

As Teresa herself said, 'I felt that separation so keenly that the feeling will not be greater, I think, when I die. For it seemed that every bone in my body was being sundered.' Nevertheless, the deed was done.

Life at the Incarnation

Faced with Teresa's 'very determined determination', as she often termed it, her father had no choice but to capitulate. He agreed to provide her with all the clothing and provisions she needed in her new life, with a dowry of goods in kind to the convent. Further, at her Profession, he would provide a guaranteed income.

The Convent of the Incarnation had moved to its present site in 1515, the year of Teresa's birth. It was a spacious building, but with an unfinished choir roof that let in the sun, rain and snow as the nuns recited the Divine Office. When she entered, there were about one hundred and fifty nuns in the community and life was fairly chaotic, despite an austere way of life. There was no enclosure, so the professed nuns were free to come and go as they wished to visit or even stay with friends and relatives - something that was vital for many of the sisters who often went hungry. Visitors and children were allowed to stay inside the convent with the nuns, who could even have their own maids.

Teresa found convent life suited her. As a novice, life was stricter than it would be later on, so she followed the monastic timetable, carried out menial tasks such as dusting and sweeping, and slept in a dormitory with the other novices. The only thing that spoiled her happiness was being corrected or not being esteemed enough. When she made her Profession two years later on 3rd November 1537, as a member of the nobility she used the title of Doña, and was given a suite of her own. This was on two levels, connected by a staircase, and included a guest room, oratory and kitchen. With her lively, witty conversation, good looks and breeding, in the parlour she soon found herself the centre of a wide circle of friends.

Illness

However, her health had not improved. With increasing fevers and fainting spells she was diagnosed to be suffering from consumption, so that in the following autumn her father arranged for her to be treated by a faith healer in Becedas. She stopped at her uncle Pedro's house. He gave her a book on prayer, *The Third Spiritual Alphabet* by Francisco de Osuna; she then went on to stay for a few months at her sister Maria's house in Castellanos de Cañada. She devoured the book. She had been struggling to pray, wanting to go beyond the vocal prayer that was all that was expected of her, but not knowing how. The sisters were not given formal teaching in mental prayer at the Incarnation; indeed, in some quarters it was considered dangerous, especially for women. Her problem was that at this point she did not understand that the mind could be plagued with distractions at a surface level, yet still be rooted in God at a deeper level. Osuna taught her to ignore distractions, to remain in peaceful, alert quietness before God. Distractions in prayer are part of the human condition: as the Lord was to remind her rather succinctly later on, 'Teresa, you are not in heaven yet!' By the time she continued her journey to Becedas in the Spring she had attained a few moments of the prayer of quiet, and considered herself quite proficient in prayer.

She made quite a hit in Becedas, this young, beautiful, prayerful nun with an interesting illness. She acquired an even greater reputation for holiness when she persuaded the parish priest to give up the mistress he was living with and live as he should. However, the treatment proved disastrous, consisting of daily purges which caused uncontrollable vomiting, unbearable pain in her heart, and weakened her so much that her exposed and shrunken nerves caused her intense pain from head to toe. Her father brought her home, an even worse invalid than before. At one point she was pronounced dead and laid in her coffin before she came round after four days, the wax still sealing her eyelids. She was unable to move, the least touch causing her so much pain that she had to be lifted in a sheet.

Teresa insisted on returning to the convent, and spent the next three years there in the infirmary. She attributed her gradual recovery to Saint Joseph, who ever after held a special place in her devotion. She never regained full health and suffered all her life from a complexity of ailments that have been endlessly analysed. In the early stage of her life some of these were undoubtedly psychosomatic, arising from an inner conflict between the desire to live a holy, prayerful life and the attraction of a superficial life of vanity and pleasure at odds with religious life. The 'treatment' she received in Becedas would have ruined the health of the most robust person. Her doctor was also to point out to her later, somewhat acerbically, when she was a busy foundress, that staying up until 2 o'clock in the morning writing letters by the light of a candle or an oil lamp, would not improve her headaches.

Meanwhile, in the convent infirmary, she read, tried to pray, and was determined to recover. Eventually she was able to take up her former life at the centre of parlour visits, even more beautiful than ever, and now a celebrity who had been cured through the intercession of Saint Joseph.

Interior conflicts and warnings

The next three years were a time of conflict for her. She was assured that the sometimes frivolous conversations she had with devout men and pious women were perfectly acceptable. This was especially so since she was drawing a certain young friar, to whom she was greatly attached, to greater devotion, just as much as he was helping her in her spiritual life. In addition, the poverty of the convent meant that popular nuns like Teresa could bring in more revenue for the community by attracting people to the parlours. After all, she was not having assignments in the church during the night as some others were! Yet deep down Teresa knew differently. She even had some experiences that warned her that the way others might behave was not for her. One day she was in the parlour with the man with whom she had formed a friendship, when she saw Our Lord glowering at her; she saw him 'with the eyes of my soul more clearly than I could have with the eyes of my body'. Another time, she saw a toad, probably jumping out from a consignment of fruit, but which scared her guilty conscience.

These experiences did not succeed in drawing her away from her pleasures and vanity. When the stress of being pulled both ways grew too great, she gave up the practice of interior prayer for a time, simply saying the vocal prayers required of her without any engagement of heart and mind. She resumed, though, when her confessor told her that that was the last thing she should do. This was even more difficult, however, because she said the Lord 'punished' her by giving her pleasure in prayer, while she still enjoyed her worldly lifestyle. The problem was that she was outgoing, enjoyed life, and loved to please people and bask in their esteem. These were all gifts of character, given her by God, but which she was using for her own gratification, and not for God's glory.

Pedro, a brother friar, described her as 'very gay and witty, her mouth so full of laughter, and although she behaved with a certain liberty she never stepped over the bounds of religious life'. Only in her own eyes, and in the burning purity of the presence of God, did she consider herself 'evil'. God wanted far more for her than her present life.

Conversion of heart

This state of things lasted for about eighteen years, until Teresa was nearly forty. It was a battle which she described as a conflict between friendship with God and friendship with the world.

The crisis came to a head when one day, in Lent 1554, she passed through an oratory and saw a statue of the wounded Christ (still preserved in the convent). Teresa said that her grief at seeing the statue and realising what Christ had gone through for her, was so great that 'I threw myself down before Him in a tremendous flood of tears, pleading with Him to give me strength, once and for all, not to sin against Him any more'.

It was a conversion as profound as that of Saint Augustine, whose *Confessions* she read soon after. She swiftly attained the prayer of quiet, and even of union, but this brought problems of its own. She sought the advice of competent confessors and directors in the spiritual life, and was often badly advised. The Carmelites she found too uneducated, the Dominicans did not want to get involved with a woman who might prove to be too much of a handful, a dangerous *illuminata*. The solution was to pass her over to the newly arrived Jesuits, whom the Dominicans considered upstarts, neither secular priests nor monks. If anything went wrong, then both could fall together.

The young, newly ordained and somewhat simple Fr Cetina was given as her confessor, and proved more competent than expected. Francisco de Salcedo was also an advisor, a wealthy layman and a friend of the family, and Gaspar Daza, a popular preacher whom Francisco had persuaded to meet Teresa, considered that for one who had only recently given up a frivolous lifestyle, to be experiencing what appeared to be advanced stages of prayer was an illusion and of the devil. Fr Cetina, on the other hand, reassured her that what she was experiencing was genuine.

With angels or men

Meanwhile, many of the nuns at the Incarnation were not at all happy about Teresa's newfound fervour, and her less frequent visits to the parlour. Salcedo decided that she should go and stay with Doña Guiomar de Ulloa, a young and wealthy widow. Guiomar, whom Teresa always called Yomar, and who remained a good friend, was enthusiastically pious and liked to amass holy people at her house, so she was pleased to add Teresa to her collection. It suited Teresa, too, and she spent some three years there. Yomar's house was well supplied with oratories, and she had greater privacy and space in which to pray. She was also able to draw on the wisdom of Yomar's Jesuit confessor, Juan de Pradanos. His main concern was Teresa's male friendships. He advised her to pray the *Veni Creator Spiritus* to ask God's guidance in the matter. She spent the day in prayer, then had her first rapture, in which she heard the words, 'Now I want you to speak not with men but with angels'. This was not meant literally; Teresa retained her love of friendship, but now God's friendship was paramount, and all her dealings seen in the light of God.

Visions and prayer

She needed the advice and direction of priests like de Pradanos, because she began to experience more and more supernatural favours such as raptures, locutions and visions. She was advised to resist and even make a rude gesture, a 'fig', but the more she obediently tried to resist them, the more they increased. This caused her great distress, because it was impossible for her to resist, and even more because she was afraid that she would be brought to the attention of the Inquisition, as several false visionaries had been. Fortunately, she was able to draw on the experience and reassurance of two saints, the Franciscan Peter of Alcantara, and Francis Borgia, the great reformer. These two assured her that her experiences were of God. She also met and had as her new confessor a young priest, Baltasar Alvarez, wise beyond his years, who was able to guide and encourage her.

In this period following her conversion, Teresa described her way of prayer. Because, as she said, she could not reflect discursively with her intellect, she liked to picture Jesus, especially in his agony on the garden - when he was most alone, and 'strove to be His companion there'. For many years this had been her custom before going to sleep. As she began to enjoy Jesus' company more she was drawn to the solitude in which she could seek him. For her, prayer was 'nothing else than an intimate sharing between friends; it means taking time frequently to be alone with Him who we know loves us.' As she began to place herself in his presence, or while reading, 'a feeling of the presence of God would come upon me unexpectedly so that I could in no way doubt He was within me or I totally immersed in Him'.

In an unusual aside, she says that she thought she had to seek seclusion in order to pray. As she makes clear, this is true, but she was beginning to discover that prayer was not limited to these times of solitary prayer, vital as these were. She was discovering the presence of Christ whatever she was doing, wherever she was, even 'among the pots and pans'.

This was an essential understanding, because, reading books on prayer, she had been given the impression that in the higher stages of prayer the sacred humanity of Jesus had to be left behind and could even be a distraction. One vision she had told her differently. Such visions and locutions, she emphasises, were with the 'inner' spiritual eye or hearing, not physical or auditory. Teresa told how one day she had a vision of Christ's hands, beautiful beyond description, and how, over the next few days, the whole of Christ's person was revealed to her. Throughout her exceptional progress to the heights of prayer and union with God, this remained its basic and unchanging reality - friendship with Christ. From then on, she was absolutely adamant that the sacred humanity of Christ was our only entry into the Trinity, into the very life of God.

Her experiences of the Risen Christ seen in inner vision became even more intense, culminating in her first experience of the transverberation, portrayed in Bernini's famous sculpture, when an angel mystically thrust a burning spear into her. The intense penetration of the love of God into her very being was experienced in her body as well, because, as she pointed out, we are, after all, body as well as soul and spirit.

In describing her progress in prayer, Teresa told what had happened to her and what the usual stages of prayer generally are. She gives the example of watering a garden. The hard way is drawing water from a well, the stage of beginners; the second way is by means of a water wheel or aqueduct, which needs less effort. The third way is by a stream or river which waters the ground around. The best way of all is when God sends rain from heaven, where all is direct gift. After the years of hard struggle in prayer, Teresa was experiencing the direct gifts of God, and said that she made more progress in a few months than in seventeen years of struggle.

She also compared the transformation of the soul to that of the caterpillar into a butterfly - Teresa herself was now taking wings.

Saint Joseph's: the first Convent

On her return to the Incarnation, Teresa found the convent just as difficult a milieu as always in which to pursue a serious life of prayer. Also, she was increasingly concerned at the news of the spread of Protestantism throughout Europe, and, from her brothers in the New World, news of millions who had never heard of Christ. So it was that one day in September 1560, she was in her rooms at the Incarnation with Juana Suárez, two young nieces who were staying with her at the convent and some cousins. They were sitting on the floor, on cushions and mats in the Moorish fashion, embroidering, and talking somewhat romantically and jokingly of the desert fathers of old. There was a deeper nostalgia within Teresa, who remembered her childhood games building hermitages. She could not help thinking of her friend Peter of Alcantara, who was busy reforming his own Franciscan order. Teresa said his unwashed body resembled old roots, he never looked at her or any woman, but he was, despite outward appearances, affable, delightful and with a lively intelligence. He lived in a tiny, basic cell, and Teresa's quarters were palatial by contrast; already she was yearning for greater simplicity.

Idea for a new Convent

At this point Yomar arrived and what had been a joke became serious. She immediately and enthusiastically offered to fund a foundation. Teresa back-tracked cautiously, until she began to receive several affirmations from the Lord that it was indeed what he wanted; he told her that the new foundation would bring great glory to him and was to be dedicated to Saint Joseph. She discussed this with her new confessor, Fr Baltasar Alvarez, who was not at all impressed with her latest enthusiasm, and referred her to her own Carmelite Provincial, Gregorio Fernández.

Seventeen years earlier, when Teresa was at a low ebb spiritually, Teresa's father had died. Although at that time Don Alonzo was outstripping his daughter spiritually, he had recognised her business acumen and appointed her his trustee. The complexities of working through family claims and demands had honed Teresa's negotiating skills and given her an insight into business and worldly affairs that now stood her in good stead as she laid plans for the new foundation. If Our Lord's saying that we should be wise as serpents and innocent as doves applied to anyone, it applied to Teresa. She amassed her spiritual big guns in Peter Alacantara and Francis Borgia, and another saint, Luis Beltrán in support of the convent. Her sister and brother-in-law, Juana and Juan de Ovalle were to look for a suitable house and buy it in their own name.

Meanwhile, Teresa herself kept a low profile. As she explained, she was not well liked in her convent, and many of the nuns considered it an insult and a poor reflection on them that she should seek a stricter life. She was deemed unstable by some, and the city itself felt that they had more than enough religious houses in Avila as it was. They would be even more opposed when they found out that Teresa wanted her convent to be founded on poverty, not as a matter necessity, but out of choice: it would be without endowments and depend on almsgiving and the work of the sisters. On the positive side, both King Philip of Spain and the Holy See were keen to reform the religious orders, although Philip wanted to do it in his own way.

Opposition

Things soon began to go wrong and the city was in an uproar. When it was discovered that Yomar was putting money towards the foundation it was also discovered that she was not as wealthy as had been thought, and debts she had accumulated began to be called in. However, if she could no longer help financially, she had influence. Teresa sent her to the Provincial to obtain the necessary permissions, and then on to Rome. Her brother-in-law had found a tiny house for them and the deeds were about to be signed when the Provincial, under pressure from the townspeople, withdrew his grudging permission. He then ordered Teresa to go to Toledo to stay with Doña Luisa de la Cerda, one of the wealthiest women in Spain. She had recently lost her husband and was grieving deeply, and it was hoped that Teresa could help her. Nothing is by chance in God's plan of things, and Doña Luisa, as well as other influential people Teresa met there, were to help her greatly later on.

Some months before, her confessor had ordered Teresa to write an account of her life and her experiences in prayer. She finished the first draft while in Toledo. This first draft was lost, but Teresa worked on it again later, adding more chapters and detail while at St Joseph's.

For years she had been giving meticulous accounts of her prayer and her spiritual experiences to a succession of confessors. She was anxious to know whether she was being deceived, emphasising that she was but an ignorant woman.

Of God or the devil

How, for example, could she tell whether a locution was of God or not? She had locutions from the devil, but the experience was totally different. Locutions from God left her spiritually strong, at peace, even when rebuked by the Lord. Those from the devil left her uneasy, guilty, disturbed in spirit, and with no inner peace. So adept did she become at distinguishing between the two, that soon, far from fearing the devil, a major preoccupation among the devout at that time, she laughed at his clumsy attempts to deceive her.

How then could she know whether her ever increasing raptures were from God or not? In Spain especially, there were religious movements going under the general name of the *alumbrados*, the enlightened. These movements arose in response to a legitimate need to grow into a deeper prayer life and union with God. But they could have dangerous effects: some devotees pursued abandonment to God, an ideal praiseworthy in itself. Saint Therese, a Carmelite of the nineteenth century, expounded it in its purest form in her teaching on the '*Little Way*'. However, understood incorrectly, this could lead to rejecting any exterior devotion, the practice of external works or self-discipline, and resulting in complete passivity. The most extreme form believed that having attained union with God one could not sin - so that any perversion became legitimate. There was also a reliance on mystical phenomena such as visions, locutions, raptures, such as experienced by Teresa. But these phenomena could be and often were a pretence and too much reliance placed on them.

As far removed as Teresa's experiences in prayer might seem, there are many similarities between her time and the present. People today still hunger for meaning in their lives, for spirituality, but often the search can lead to a desire for spiritual experiences for their own sake, divorced from the moral imperatives of holiness of life and a moral and ethical foundation.

Teresa's answer may not be popular in our individualistic age with its distrust of authority. She was unswerving in her search for the best spiritual directors and guides she could find, who were rooted and trained in the fifteen centuries of wisdom and tradition of the Catholic Church in its teaching on prayer, the spiritual life and doctrine. Before all else, she knew that true spirituality resulted in obedience to the will of God, in humility, holiness and peace of soul. Rooting herself in that rich tradition, she herself became an outstanding part of it, a teacher of the spiritual life to countless others who have followed her since. 'After all,' Teresa declared, 'I am a daughter of the Church'.

The new foundation

In June 1562, the Provincial rescinded his order keeping Teresa in Toledo; Doña Luisa sulked at losing her favourite nun and refused to provide her with an escort back to Avila. Instead, Juan de Ovalle came to collect her. On their arrival in Avila they found Peter of Alcantara with the brief from Rome in his hands. It authorised Teresa to make the foundation, and to draw up statutes for it, thus overriding her Provincial, and placing the foundation under the jurisdiction of the Bishop of Avila. Opposition, which had been dormant, now flared up again, but providentially Juan fell ill, and of course Teresa had to look after him in the little house earmarked for the foundation. They could then quietly make it ready as a convent. It was poor enough. Teresa brought with her a cracked bell, an altar, straw for some beds, and statues of Our Lady and Saint Joseph.

The convent was opened on 24th August, with four women entering as the founding sisters, but without Teresa. Although she attended the first Mass celebrated there, Teresa did not have the necessary permission to transfer from the Incarnation. However, Teresa herself gave the coarse habit of the Reform to the new candidates whom she called her 'four poor orphans'. Leaving them there to their own devices, without any idea of how to live the religious life, was a wrench and a deep worry for her, but the Lord reassured her that all would be well. All she lacked was courage and trust.

She needed both when she witnessed the reaction as the cracked bell rang out for that first Mass in St Joseph's. Townsfolk rushed out as if there was a fire and declared their children would have to starve to feed the four women. They besieged the house to drag the nuns out, but they barricaded themselves in while workmen tried to tear down the doors. The authorities declared that the convent would exhaust the city's water supply. The matter was then dragged through the courts. Eventually things died down, and a few people began to enjoy attending Mass at the poor little convent. Then in December, Teresa and some nuns were given permission to transfer from the Incarnation to St Joseph's. At the beginning of the New Year 1563, Teresa became the Prioress of her community.

Life at St Joseph's

So began a period for Teresa that was perhaps the happiest of her life. She had founded St Joseph's so that she and her nuns could follow the original Rule of Saint Albert, without mitigation. This Rule had been given to a group of laymen in the 13th Century. During the Crusades they had settled on Mount Carmel, and wanted to lead a life of prayer. When the Holy Land was captured again by the Muslims, the Carmelites, as they were called, had to leave and settle in Europe, joining the other mendicant orders such as the Franciscans, that were springing up at that time. Over the years, this simple Rule had been altered from its original austerity, to take account of changing needs, and especially of the devastation wrought by the Black Death that had ravaged Europe. As Teresa had discovered at the Incarnation, the original simplicity of the Carmelite life had been overlaid by so many changes that she wanted to strip these additions away to reveal its original purpose.

Now she had the poverty, simplicity, silence and seclusion she needed for deepening her prayer life - the very thing that the Carmelite Rule was designed to foster.

Beginnings

She drew up a well-balanced timetable for her nuns that combined prayer with work, periods of silence and two periods of recreation which Teresa was adamant were vital for the spiritual and mental health of her daughters. There were times for singing and laughter and sisterly chat while they worked. Visits to the parlour were strictly regulated, and not given to frivolous conversation. Teresa herself took her spinning to the parlour, which annoyed her old friend Francisco de Salcedo. He said that if she would please not spin while they were talking, he would give her the money that she would have earned from her labours.

She now had to train her nuns in the life she had drawn up for them. Much of it was in contrast to the life she had lived in the Incarnation. At first, the community was limited to thirteen nuns, but when this proved impractical the number was increased to twenty-one, and then in our own times, to twenty five. She wanted her community to be a family, bonded together by sisterly love. This did not mean that there were no tensions. Of the first four nuns, Antonia del Espiritu Santo had an unhealthy liking for bodily mortification. Ursula do los Santos had been a woman about town, Maria de Avila was sweet and childlike; Maria de la Cruz had been one of Yomar's servants. None had any experience of religious life, although they were soon joined by a few experienced nuns from the Incarnation. The first Prioress was Ana de San Juan, who was harsh and liked to humiliate the sisters. Fortunately, she soon preferred the comforts of the Incarnation to the austerities of Saint Joseph, and returned there, leaving Teresa free to be elected as Prioress.

Poverty

Teresa had wanted her convent to be founded in poverty and there was indeed great privation. They lived mainly on bread, cheese and fruit, with an egg or a sardine as a luxury. At first, the nuns went barefoot (or 'discalced', in contrast to the 'calced' or shod nuns of the Incarnation), but when the harsh climate of Castile made this imprudent, they wore coarse sandals of hemp, called *alpargates*.

Teresa encouraged her daughters to meet the hardships of their life with valour and above all with that indispensable quality in monastic life: a sense of humour. The sisters duly obliged. When they voted to exchange the linen tunics under their habits for a coarser wool, they were concerned that they might be infested with lice. They therefore added a stanza to a song Teresa had composed, begging the lice to stay away - which they duly did.

Teacher of prayer

In contrast to the elaborate and protracted celebration of the prayers of the Divine Office at the Incarnation, in Carmels of the Reform the liturgy would be celebrated simply, sung or chanted in a monotone. This enabled the nuns to spend more time in personal prayer, at least two hours a day. Teresa had learnt from her own experience how vital to the spiritual life was this time set aside for meditation and contemplative prayer, nourished by daily celebration of the Mass and the Church's liturgy.

To help the sisters grow in prayer, Teresa wrote another of her masterpieces, *The Way of Perfection*. In it she stressed that they had come to St Joseph's not only for their own perfection but to pray for the Church and for the world. Theirs was to be an apostolic vocation. 'O my sisters in Christ!' she exclaimed: 'Help me in my supplications before the Lord. For this He has gathered you together here; this is your vocation; these are your affairs; these must be your desires, the object of your tears; these your petitions, and not, my sisters, for the interests of the world'.

Recalling her own struggles in prayer, when she had dreaded the thought of the hour set aside for meditation, and how she had longed for the hour to be up, now she wanted her nuns to understand the ways of prayer, and how to progress in it. Since prayer is friendship with Christ, she wanted her nuns to be good nuns: 'My whole desire was and is still, since He has so many enemies and so few friends, that these last should be good.' If we can be judged by the company we keep, then those seeking a life of prayer have to grow more like their friend. So it is no accident that at least a third of the book is taken up with practical teaching on growing in that likeness, before Teresa even begins to talk about prayer itself. Her standards are high, and if her nuns say 'we're no angels, we are not saints', that is no excuse. 'Remember that though we are not, it is well to think, that God helping us, we could, if we made the effort, become so.'

Teresa recognised that not everyone is called to contemplation, though all are called to meditation and mental prayer. She does not despise vocal prayer, since if our thoughts are on God while we recite them, then we are praying, and that could even lead to contemplation. 'I am not asking you now to think about Him, nor to produce many reflections, nor that you make long and studied meditations with your understanding. I do not ask you to do more than look at Him. Now who is there to prevent you from turning the eyes of your soul, though it be for a moment if you can do no more, upon this Lord? You can look at very ugly things; can you not look upon the most beautiful object imaginable?' She then sets her teaching in the context of the greatest of prayers: the Our Father.

As for Teresa's own prayer, her raptures and ecstasies became more frequent, so the sisters became quite relaxed about them. When she levitated, Teresa would cling on to the choir grilles in a vain attempt to prevent it; the sisters would grab hold of her habit in an equally vain attempt to restrain her.

The convent was a square and unpretentious building, with a small and lovely garden where the sisters could grow flowers, fruit and vegetables. It delighted Teresa, who could easily raise her mind and heart amidst beauty. She had a few little hermitages built in the garden, where she and the sisters could go for even greater solitude. Unfortunately, Lázaro Dávila, the local water inspector, decided that the little hermitages posed a severe threat to the city's water supply, by blocking the sunlight so that the water would freeze in winter. Teresa had to go to court to contest the ridiculous assertion, but without success, and the hermitages were knocked down. Teresa simply rebuilt them in another, more secluded part of the garden.

As this affair showed, the foundation was still resented by some elements within Avila. In the convent however, Teresa, with her generous heart, wisdom and common sense, forged a little community where harmony and peace reigned.

A new mission

In 1566, the Pope issued a papal bull ordering all communities of women to observe enclosure. To this end, the Prior General of the Carmelites, Giovanni Battista Rossi, always known as Rubeo, came to Spain to inspect all the houses. By the time he reached Avila and Saint Joseph's he had had a bruising and fruitless journey inspecting the Andalusian houses that were dissolute and where abuses were rife. He was surprised, relieved and delighted to find at Saint Joseph's a house that met all his aims. He admired the poverty and simplicity he found there, although he was not inclined to emulate their example himself - he travelled with a retinue that included a valet, a cook, a secretary, a laundryman, a barber, several assistants, and grooms for his horses.

Teresa awaited his arrival with some trepidation and with determination, because she had plans to set before him. A Franciscan friar had arrived from the New World telling them of the thousands of Indians who did not know of Christ. Teresa's zeal was on fire, wishing she were a man so that she could go there herself. In tears of longing, she heard the Lord say to her, 'Wait a little, daughter, and you will see great things.' With new vocations knocking at her door, she wanted to found more houses. She found a ready ear in Rubeo. He was so impressed with what he found in Saint Joseph's that he told her to found as many houses as the hairs on her head. The only proviso was that she found them in Castile, not Andalusia, which might prove too hard a nut to crack. She also obtained permission to found two houses of friars. Her time of seclusion and peace was at an end.

First Foundations

For the next twenty years of her life, Teresa was to be almost constantly on the move, founding sixteen more monasteries, in addition to Saint Joseph's. For someone in the best of health this would have been a daunting task, but Teresa was never a well woman. So her achievement is even more impressive, especially given the state of travel in those days. The roads were atrocious or almost non-existent; journeys would be taken often in the sweltering heat of summer or the bitter cold of winter. The nuns would usually travel in a covered wagon, where - as far as possible - they would follow the Carmelite day of prayer, the Divine Office and recreation. Teresa would also instruct them in the Carmelite way of life. Sometimes journeys would be made by mule or horseback. Sometimes a wealthy patron would supply a carriage, but when Teresa was rebuked by a priest one day for arriving in one, she avoided them unless absolutely necessary.

They would be escorted by their friars or other men to guard them against bandits, and when they arrived at an inn, against the unwelcome attentions of the uncouth men drinking there. The inns were another source of extreme discomfort that Teresa dreaded and avoided if she could.

Often there would be little or no food; the beds would be bug-infested; their nights disturbed by the raucous drinking below.

Trials and troubles

Drawing on her experience of founding Saint Joseph's, Teresa knew her task would never be easy, and the way she set about it in subsequent foundations follows a similar pattern. She knew there would be opposition from townsfolk who already had more than enough religious houses to cope with. Equally, the other settled communities of nuns would object to another foundation that could take revenue away from them. Teresa was adamant that she wanted her houses to be founded in poverty; that is, while she had to find the money to buy a house in the first place, and postulants would provide a dowry, she did not want her monasteries to have endowments that would provide them with an on-going revenue. This sometimes proved impossible; so she did on occasion have to compromise, although poverty remained her ideal.

Permission would have to be sought to make the foundation, and here Teresa proved adroit. There was often conflict over the authorities who were entitled to give the necessary permission: the Carmelite fathers, or the bishop, or by indult from Rome, or again the secular authorities. Each could be played off against another; a verbal expression of interest could be interpreted as authority to go ahead; if there was a conflict, Teresa could produce documentation from the highest authority she had at any given moment. If there were irate sensibilities to placate, then she could rely on her charm and wit to bring the authorities round to her way of thinking.

Next, would be the question of buying a house - often with the scantiest of means. Here, the contacts she had made while staying with Doña Luis de la Cerda paid off. These highborn ladies felt there was something quite romantic about living in poverty, provided that they were not the ones to do it. It was quite something to be the benefactor behind a foundation, and they could even provide a house on occasion. Often this would be so tumbledown that no-one else would live in it.

Then the foundation had to be established. Because of the anticipated opposition, Teresa tried to arrange things so that the sisters would arrive during the night and even set up a makeshift chapel where Mass could be said in the morning. Once the chapel had been consecrated with the Mass, it could not easily be undone.

The first foundation Teresa made (after Saint Joseph's) was at Medina del Campo, and this met with all these problems. Teresa chose this town, not too far away, because a good friend and one of her more sympathetic confessors, Baltasar Alvarez, had just been made rector there, and could provide help and support. Julian de Avila, the chaplain at

Saint Joseph's, together with a Carmelite friar, Fr Antonio de Heredia, found a house for them to rent, which was just as well as she had no money to buy one.

Six nuns were found to make the foundation with Teresa. On their way there, they had news that the landlord would not let them enter the house until they had received permission from a nearby Augustinian priory. The nuns had to be dropped off at the houses of relatives, leaving Julian of Avila, Teresa and two of the nuns to go on ahead. Fr Antonio had found a wealthy lady with a house to sell for almost nothing; she did not even want a deposit. This should have rung alarm bells but Teresa was only too pleased that they could proceed with their plans.

The little band arrived around midnight at Medina and roused the Carmelite friars so they could give them the necessary vessels and vestments to say Mass. Then nuns, priests and friars crept through the streets as if they had robbed a church, running the gauntlet of thugs who made 'the kind of remarks expected of them'. The house was in the sort of state that Teresa came to expect. Half of it was uninhabitable: plaster crumbled off the walls, there was dust, rubble and dirt everywhere. They spent the night making a corner of it as habitable as possible and a cracked bell rang out at dawn to announce that Mass was being celebrated. They then had to rouse the notary from his bed so that the legalities could be sorted out, and the foundation was made. The other nuns were summoned to

join them, and the little community stayed with a
benefactor until their house was ready for them.

Friars

While she was at Medina, Teresa began to make plans for
her convent of friars. She talked the idea over with Fray
Antonio, and she was quite startled when he immediately
offered himself. Teresa knew that the middle-aged friar
liked his well-appointed cell and his creature comforts, and
she doubted that he would be able to adapt to the rigours of
the Discalced life. Then, a young friar came to see her in
the parlour: a swarthy, prematurely balding man, short in
stature, with burning brown eyes. His name was Fray Juan
de Santo Matia. After talking to him, and discerning the
depths of his spirituality and union with God, she was
convinced that she now had a friar and a half.

A dilapidated house at Duruelo was found for the two
of them and a lay brother, and within a few months the
first house of Discalced friars was established. Taking the
habit, Fray Juan de Santo Matia changed his name, and
would thereafter be known as John of the Cross, poet and
mystic, later to become a Saint and Doctor of the Church.

Troubles ahead

Earlier, Doña Luisa de la Cerda, Duchess of Alba, had
heard of the Medina foundation and decided she would
like one too, at Malagón, so that the nuns could offer

prayers for her dead husband. A laudable aim, but the burden put a great strain on the nuns. She was a bit of a problem: she sulked and withdrew if she discovered Teresa had other patrons, once leaving the nuns who were founding a house in Toledo cold, hungry and destitute until another kind benefactor came to their rescue. On the other hand, another benefactor, Doña Maria, provided a lavish house and endowment in Valladolid, so that Teresa had to choose nuns who were sufficiently robust to live the simplicity of the Rule in such a setting. Her niece, Maria Bautista, became its autocratic Prioress. As Teresa once remarked, 'These founders of mine are full of tricks'. However, if Teresa thought Doña Luisa was a problem, an even greater one appeared in her cousin: Ana de Mendoza y la Cerda, the Princess of Eboli.

The troublesome princess

Ruy Gomez, Duke of Eboli, was a childhood playmate of the King, and was often sent on diplomatic missions, which, given the character of the woman he had married, suited him well. Ana had been married to him when she was twelve years old, and bore him eleven children. A portrait in which she appears shows a young woman with an eye patch, a petulant little face and a sharp expression - some said that she had lost an eye at a joust. But it did not tell all about her character. She had a ferocious temper when crossed, was vindictive, wilful and spoilt.

Teresa had heard that she wanted to found a Carmel in Pastrana. One day, as she was still establishing the Toledo convent, a carriage arrived to carry Teresa - immediately - to the princess. Teresa could see from the terrified servants that she would brook no refusal. Teresa then heard the Lord tell her that it was his will she make the foundation: when she received a locution like that, it always meant that Teresa was going to walk into a lot of difficulty, and so she did.

When the small group of founding nuns arrived at Pastrana they found that, despite the princess's haste, the convent was not yet ready. They had to spend several weeks cooped up in one room in the palace. The princess had her own ideas of poverty; as a result the building was far too small for the purpose, and they would live without income. This, according to her, would show more perfection. In other words, if the villagers could not give them alms, then they would starve. Diplomatically, Ruy Gomez undertook to provide for them if necessary out of his own pocket. The princess filled the tiny house with possessions, which Mother Isabel de Santo Domingo, who became the convent's outstanding Prioress, inventoried carefully and with foresight.

Far more humiliating for Teresa than the unsatisfactory foundation under the capricious Princess of Eboli, was that the princess had heard from Doña Luisa of Teresa's *Life*. Teresa was most reluctant to submit a copy of it, but when faced with a barrage of temper tantrums she was forced to hand over what she called 'her soul'. The princess then thumbed through it, sniggering and laughing, sharing the best titbits with her ladies in waiting, and sent off choice snippets to the court in Madrid.

Five years after the foundation was made, the prince died. The princess was histrionic in her grief, and when the funeral was over, donned a friar's habit and made her way to enter the Pastrana convent. Mother Isabel, on being forewarned, exclaimed, 'That's the end of this convent!' It nearly was. The princess had no idea of what being a nun entailed, and even if she had, was not inclined to follow it. She was also five months pregnant. She ordered everyone around as if she were the Prioress, and the nuns had to address her on their knees. 'The princess of Eboli as a nun,' remarked Teresa, 'was enough to make you weep.' Fortunately, she soon tired of being a nun and returned to her palace, but still succeeded in making the sisters' lives a misery. It was obvious that something had to be done.

Escape

Secretly plans were made to transfer the community to Segovia. A rescue party headed by Julián of Avila and Antonio Gaitán, a layman who was to be a staunch friend to Teresa, came for them. With bags packed they climbed on to donkey carts during the night and fled, leaving all the goods that belonged to the princess in the convent.

The princess had a potent weapon: the copy of Teresa's *'Life'*. In revenge, she despatched it to the Inquisition, then sat back to await results. Unfortunately for her, the Inquisition passed it on to Fr Domingo Bañez for assessment. He was a close ally and supporter of Teresa, and he approved the book; so nothing came of the princess's vindictiveness. Moreover, those who had the task of scrutinising her works were often drawn to a deeper prayer life themselves.

Teresa stayed only a few days in Pastrana before leaving Mother Isabel in charge. Soon she was off on her travels again, arriving at the end of October in Salamanca - its university was one of the most prestigious in Europe - to make another foundation. It was a cold journey and Teresa was unwell. At one point they had to cross the Arevalillo River, swollen from the autumn rains. The whole party was convinced that there was no way their wagons could make it across, apart from Teresa who pointed to one part of the river where the churning waters appeared calm. They forded the river easily at that point, but when the men turned back to look, it was just as dangerous as before.

Teresa took only one nun with her, to make it easier if things went wrong The other nuns waited to be summoned once the advance party had settled in. The party arrived, unusually, in the middle of the day, since Teresa had been assured the foundation would be easy to set up. However she found that the students who had finished their studies, were still in the property and were refusing to budge. Towards evening they finally left, angrily and unwillingly. The party had to set to and clean it thoroughly, for, as Teresa said, the students 'must not have had a gift for cleanliness'

Her companion was an older nun, Maria del Sacramento, who was of a highly nervous disposition. She was convinced that a student had stayed behind and hidden himself somewhere in the house, so the two of them locked themselves in a room, where there was straw for them to sleep on. Since the rest of the party had departed, Maria was now worried what would happen if she should die - the bells were ringing all over the city for the Vigil of All Souls. 'Sister', Teresa replied, 'when this happens, I'll think about what to do; now, let me sleep.' Both survived the night, and more nuns arrived the next day.

The Salamanca foundation was founded in 1570. By January the following year, after another foundation in Alba de Tormes, Teresa had founded eight communities of women and three communities of men. Suddenly, all this activity came to abrupt end. She received an unexpected order to return to the Convent of the Incarnation, as the new Prioress.

Storm Clouds over the Reform

Teresa divided opinion. To some, she was a holy nun and a celebrity. To others, such as Felipe Sega, the Papal Nuncio, she was 'an unstable, restless, disobedient and contumacious female.' And Teresa described herself as 'a footloose pilgrim'. She was not universally popular, not with her own Provincial, Angel de Salazar, nor with Pedro Fernandez, the apostolic visitor to Castile. So Angel devised a brilliant plan.

Sorting out disorder

Affairs at the convent of the Incarnation were worse even than in Teresa's time there. Food was so scarce that many of the nuns had moved out and lay boarders had taken their place, making it even more chaotic. Angel suggested to Fernandez that Teresa be imposed as Prioress to sort things out. Given his animosity towards her, he hoped and expected she would fail and her reputation be destroyed. Fernandez went to see Teresa himself at St Joseph's, where she now was, and came away deeply impressed by her quiet assurance, strength of character and humility, declaring that she was a 'bearded woman'! To him, if anyone could sort out the Incarnation, she could.

To return to that 'Babylon' (as she termed it) was the last thing Teresa herself wanted, but obedience demanded it. Before she entered as Prioress she ordered that all the boarders leave, which encouraged some of the nuns to return and others to be outraged. They also resented the fact she had been imposed on them and not voted in, and were fearful that she would introduce the Discalced reforms into the convent. By mid-October, when Teresa walked in procession to the convent carrying a statue of Saint Joseph as she always did, the nuns had worked themselves into a frenzy, posting men from the town in front of the door to prevent her from entering. Teresa sat quietly on a rock while the door was forced open and a way made for her, with the nuns screaming so loudly that the noise could be heard inside the city.

Teresa made her way to the Choir while the nuns screamed that they did not want her, until one voice was heard above the hubbub: 'Yes, we want her and we love her!' The stand-off was broken.

The following day the nuns were stunned when Teresa entered the Choir and (absentmindedly, they thought) took her seat, not in the Prioress's stall, but in her old stall of nine years previously. They then saw that Teresa had placed a statue of Our Lady of Mercy in the Prioress's stall, with the keys of the convent hanging from her hand; her conquest of hearts and minds had begun.

John of the Cross

She set about restoring order to the convent, sorting out the accounts, begging for donations, even from her cash-strapped sister Juana, so that the sisters would have enough to eat. She reassured them that she had no intention of imposing the Discalced Rule on them. By March she was exhausted, ill and in pain. She wrote to Maria de Mendoza, 'Any one of these ailments would have been enough to kill me if God had been pleased to desire it, but apparently He's not about to do me that favour.'

To lead the nuns into a genuine life of prayer she realised that she needed help from a priest who had the spiritual authority to win their trust. And who better to do this than Fray John of the Cross? In the years since she had first met him, she had become increasingly impressed by the depth of his holiness and wisdom. Uncompromising in his own life of prayer and self-denial, he was gaining an increasing reputation as a compassionate, gentle and understanding spiritual guide to all classes of people - beginners as much as those advanced in the spiritual life. He soon won over the sisters who feared he would be too strict. Several of the nuns testified that although they often could not take in with their minds what he was saying, they went away with a deeper consciousness of the love and presence of God, and eager to do his will. He revealed to them the burning love that God had for them;

he respected them and wanted them to go as far as they could in love of God.

As for Teresa, John felt she also could go further than she had so far. He tried to wean her, unsuccessfully, from her dependence on visions and locutions, and towards greater detachment. He felt uncomfortable with her emotionalism; his burning love for God was like a deep well within. To humble her, he once said to the nuns in her presence, 'she reveals her sins very prettily'. Then, knowing she was fond of receiving large hosts, even though she knew the Lord was present in even the smallest morsel, he divided a host in two and gave her only half. She went into ecstasy, and heard God saying to her, 'Do not fear, daughter, no one can separate you from me. Look at this iron nail, it is a sign that from now on you shall be my espoused bride. Until now you did not deserve it. From now on, think of my honour not only as that of your Creator, or of your God and King, but as if you had already truly become My bride. My honour is yours, and yours Mine.'

Salamanca

Within two years, they had created between them a happy, harmonious enough community to win the approval of Fr Fernandez. Towards the end of her three year tenure at the Incarnation, Teresa returned to the Salamanca convent, of which she was still titular

Prioress, to supervise their move into a new house. It was a journey to remember, and Julián of Avila, who escorted her with Fr Antonio, wrote a vivid account of it. As they set off, the elderly Antonio fell off his mule, and then the nun's assistant fell off her mule as well. When night came, the mule that carried Ana de Jesus' dowry, which was intended to purchase the new house, wandered off and they spent the rest of the night looking for it. There was nothing to eat when they reached one of the terrible inns, although next day they found the mule feeding by the side of the road, the dowry, remarkably, untouched.

The following night, for some reason the party split in two, and then spent a good part of the night looking for each other. When they finally arrived at an overcrowded, bug-ridden inn to try and sleep a little, Julián said that the best thing about it 'was that we longed to leave it'.

While she was at Salamanca, Teresa began writing *Foundations* at the request of Jerónimo Ripalda, her confessor. This was an account of the houses she had founded to date, although it is more than that for it contains much good advice for her prioresses and nuns.

Obedience

There was great admiration in religious circles for examples of extreme penance and mortification. In the early days of her conversion Teresa was not averse to some of it herself, on one occasion harnessing herself to a load of heavy stones. But her innate good sense made her wary of extremes. She cautioned her prioresses not to impose extra burdens on their nuns that they would not place on themselves. In *Foundations* she gives a lengthy account of one of the most famous of the penitents, Doña Catalina de Cardona, at one level extolling and even admiring her, but on another level expressing her unease: 'When I was thinking about the terrific penance performed by Doña Catalina de Cardona, and how I could have done more of it myself (the Lord had sometimes made me want to) if I hadn't been obeying my confessors, I wondered if it wouldn't be better to stop obeying them about this from now on. The Lord said to me, 'No, daughter, that's wrongheaded. You're following a good, safe path. Do you see all the penances she performs? I prize your obedience more.'

Even obedience can be overdone, though. While at St Joseph's she had handed Sr Maria Bautista a rotten cucumber and told her to plant it. 'Upright or sideways?' she asked. As a test of obedience this was harmless enough, but when a Prioress told a sister in annoyance to go and jump in the well and she started to do so, then Teresa was not amused. On another occasion a Sister showed a nun a very large worm, telling her to observe how pretty it was. The Prioress said to the nun jokingly, 'well, let Sister eat it.' She was found in the kitchen frying it, ready to eat. 'And the Prioress,' added Teresa, in

recounting this incident, 'could have done her much harm.'
Prioresses had to be very careful what orders they gave.

Despite her own illnesses, Teresa was always
solicitous of others' health, recommending an infusion of
rhubarb to one Prioress, and warning another against
taking sarsaparilla water. She touchingly admits that she
does not want to go to the Malagón Carmel because, 'For
one thing, there is no point in it, for I am neither strong
enough, nor have I charity enough, to nurse sick nuns.'

Great harvest

In addition to the concerns about her various convents,
there was also a great deal to worry about on the wider
scene. Girls were flocking to the Discalced convents,
friaries were springing up, and the Calced friars were
feeling increasingly angry and jealous about the Reform's
success. To make matters worse, the friars were going
over the Prior General's head and obtaining permission
from Rome to found houses in Andalusia, which Rubeo
had expressly forbidden them to do. For some reason he
blamed Teresa for this, even though Teresa herself
disapproved of the way these friaries were often going
their own way.

To make matters worse, she made a foundation in
Beas, which was in Castile. However, unknown to her, it
was considered for ecclesiastical purposes as being in
Andalusia. As she explained in a long letter to Rubeo,

'Your Reverence must also know that I made enquiries everywhere before coming to Beas, so as to be sure it was not Andalusia, where I had not the slightest intention of making a foundation, as I do not care for the people.' She had been there for over a month before she realised the true situation, and by then she could not abandon the foundation. Rubeo would not be mollified.

Fray Jeronimo

Nevertheless, Teresa enjoyed her time in Beas. She said it was delightful with a good climate - and it proved momentous for her. In April of that year, 1575, she met for the first time Fray Jerónimo de la Madre de Díos - Gracián, Apostolic Visitor to the Calced Carmelites of Andalusia, although he himself was Discalced. Teresa was enchanted. He was thirty at the time, and had risen rapidly through the ranks of the Discalced. He had all the qualities Teresa admired. A slightly plump man, he was scholarly, highly gifted, spiritual and diplomatic. He had the same charm that Teresa had, and to her he was the perfect religious. She found that she could open up her soul to him completely, and flatteringly, he opened up his soul to her in a way she had never experienced before. A few weeks after their first meeting, she made a vow of obedience to him.

She was soon writing enthusiastically about him to Mother Inés de Jesús, Prioress of Medina, 'Oh, Mother, how much I have wished you were here with me during these last few days! I must tell you that, without exaggeration, I think they have been the best days of my life. For over three weeks we have had Father-Master Gracián here; and, much as I have had to do with him, I assure you I have not yet fully realised his worth. To me, he is perfect.' Also, 'He is such a pleasing man, so tender and agreeable that no-one can find anything wrong with him' she wrote again. Teresa could not, but others could, and she wrote vehemently to her cousin Maria Bautista, who was not impressed with him, to defend him: 'If your Reverence finds fault in him, it will be because you seldom see him or have anything to do with him. I assure you he is a saintly man, and not in the least headstrong, but very cautious.'

Seville foundation

How cautious, she was soon to find out, when he ordered her to make a foundation in Seville. They set out in the heat of an Andalusian summer, May 1575, that made their covered wagons veritable ovens. Teresa had a high fever, fights broke out in the dreadful inns they were forced to stay at, and they consoled themselves by thinking of hell. Even so, they managed to keep the good humour that never seemed to be in short supply during their journeys.

When they arrived in Seville they found that the Bishop had not given them the license for the foundation. Gracián, from Madrid, had to smooth things over, because he had assumed Mariano, a friend of the Bishop, had obtained the license. The house found for them was in a poor condition, damp and unpleasant, and neighbours who had loaned them a few household items descended to take them back again. Seville was a wealthy city, but it was the meanest Teresa had been to. Fortunately Teresa's brother Lorenzo returned from Peru in August, and was so appalled at the state of the house they were forced to live in that he found them a new property - with walls 'like frosted sugar' as Teresa described them.

Worse was to come. One of the nuns, Maria del Corro, had been admitted against Teresa's better judgement through powerful friends she had. She found that convent life did not suit her, and made claims against Teresa to the Inquisition. Its officers arrived at the convent, but found the aged 61 year old foundress was quite different from the temptress they had been led to expect; the accusations were so far-fetched that they left her in peace.

Rubeo, however, did not leave her in peace, despite the long letters she wrote to him explaining her situation, and trying to convince him that she had never wanted to disobey him. In December, Teresa received orders from him to retire to a Castilian Carmel of her choice and stay there. Her constant travelling was causing scandal, and Rome was tightening up the rules about nuns leaving their convents. Gracián, hearing of the order, gave her a different order, to stay in Seville for the winter because of her health. She eventually left in June the following year.

Closing years

Teresa was at last back in Castile, in Toledo, the convent of her choice. She wrote to her brother that she had 'a very nice cell, extremely secluded, with a window overlooking the garden'.

More writing

In this quiet cell she began work on another of Gracián's commands. Teresa's *Life* was still with the Inquisition, so Gracián asked her to continue writing, especially on the subject of prayer. It was a test of Teresa's vow of obedience, because, as she said, she did not have the inclination for the task and her health was not good. 'I have been experiencing now for three months such great noise and weakness in my head that I've found it a hardship even to write concerning necessary business matters'. Then she received the image of a palace of crystal, and understood how she could use it as the basis for her exposition. So she began the book, *The Interior Castle*, on the Feast of the Trinity. What began as a chore ended as a delight. Each time she began to write she would pray to the Holy Spirit to guide her pen, and her nuns testified that He did indeed do that. She often wrote at great speed, her face radiant, and an expression of intense prayer as she experienced what she was describing.

The Interior Castle

Years before, shortly before her conversion, Teresa had a vision of hell, in which she found herself confined in a tiny, noisome hole. For a soul as expansive as Teresa's, to be confined like this would truly be hell. But this generosity and expansiveness of spirit was a charism not for herself alone, but a legacy to be passed on to her daughters and to all who would learn from her. Even externally she wanted her Carmels to be spacious and pleasant, which was why she was so distressed at the paucity of the Princess of Eboli's provision. Even so, while a Carmelite is restricted in her surroundings, there is no limit to her spiritual dwelling, which is no less than the palace of the King of kings.

Seven mansions

This palace or castle Teresa sees as consisting of seven rooms or mansions, leading from the outside inwards towards the innermost room where God dwells. She describes the outer rooms where there were snakes and vipers of worldliness and distractions. Did she realise that those years when she felt herself far from God were in reality the first steps in her journey to the indwelling of God within her deepest being?

Worsening health

On Christmas Eve, Teresa fell down some stairs and broke her left arm. It was badly set and had to be reset a few months later; still she lost the use of that arm, and was in continual pain from it. Teresa was by this time chronically sick, but her broken arm had brought her a great treasure in the shape of a young lay sister, Ana de San Bartolomé, who from now on was her constant companion, secretary and nurse.

How did she cope with all these trials? She gives some hints in *The Interior Castle* which she had completed in November. 'Keep your eyes on the Crucified, and all these things will be small.' Despite her intense distress, because all she wanted was the will of God to be done, she explained how souls 'have a great interior joy when they are persecuted, with much more peace than that mentioned, and without any hostile feelings toward those who do, or desire to do, them evil. On the contrary, such a soul gains a particular love for its persecutors.' Surely she was speaking from her own experience.

Teresa finished *The Interior Castle* with joy and praise. She had discovered that whatever her trials, no-one could take her Castle from her. 'May God our Lord be forever praised and blessed, amen, amen'.

By this time she was in Avila, having been given permission to travel there to deal with business matters at St Joseph's. Because of her worsening health she stayed there for over a year. Rubeo might have thought she was down, but she was not out. She kept up a lively correspondence with the prioresses of all her many convents. This was not limited to business matters. Her niece, Sr Teresa of Jesus in Avila, had problems with bad thoughts about another sister. 'Try not to think about it - just turn your mind away. Don't think you are doing wrong when a bad thought comes to you - wish for her own good. Make the sign of the Cross and try to think of something else.' 'I wish you had a larger kitchen garden,' she wrote to Mother María de San José in Seville with her customary common sense, 'so that Beatriz could have more to do' - the sister in question had an excess of imagination, and a bit more manual work would do her good.

Discalced province

Gracián, who was determined that there should eventually be a separate Discalced province, came to visit her and work out a strategy. Both of them enjoyed a bit of intrigue, so they worked out a form of code they could use when writing to each other in case their correspondence was intercepted. Teresa was 'Angela' or 'Laurencia', Gracián was 'Paul' or 'Eliseo'. The Discalced friars were 'eagles', the nuns 'butterflies', while the Calced were 'cats' or 'owls'.

There were complicated negotiations, and ill will on both sides, with the hapless Gracián attacked and denigrated and even excommunicated for a time. At last on 1st April 1579, the King established the Discalced Carmelites as a separate province, so bringing some peace. This was mostly accomplished by Nicolás Doria, a Genovise banker who had joined the Order two years previously, and who proved a skilful negotiator. Teresa was beginning to recognise that Gracián did have some weaknesses and shortcomings, and that she could not always depend on him, so she was delighted with her new acquisition. It was fortunate that she died before Doria showed his true colours and, later on, nearly wrecked the Reform.

More new convents

The following month, Angel de Salazar, the new vicar general, gave Teresa permission to continue founding more convents. She wasted no time, because she also wanted to visit some of the Carmels already founded and which had problems. Opinion was still divided about Teresa - was she saint or deluded sinner? On the journey to Malagón she was mobbed by admirers, who held up their children for her blessing. But in one town she was almost attacked for her 'immorality', which the townsfolk thought had been responsible for the Inquisition's visitation.

She went on to Toledo where she became seriously ill from the influenza that was sweeping the country. She survived, but her brother Lorenzo did not, nor did her good friend Baltazar Alvarez. As she remarked sadly to Mother María de San José, 'I'm four years older than my brother was, and I never manage to die.' She was very depressed for a while, but gradually her spirits recovered, and with it a new serenity. She rarely had ecstasies now, but a continual intellectual awareness of the indwelling of the Trinity within her. People often commented on a pleasing perfume that emanated from her.

In September 1581, she arrived in Avila to sort out the affairs of Saint Joseph's, which were in a bad way. Lorenzo's will, in which he had left money to the convent, was being contested by the family, and the nuns were finding it difficult to survive. When she arrived they elected Teresa as their Prioress - 'You would think I had nothing else to keep me busy!' she exclaimed.

In November John of the Cross came to visit her, hoping to take her with him to make a foundation in Granada. Teresa, however, had had a locution that she should make a foundation in Burgos, and despite John arguing with her all evening she would not be budged. He took instead Mother Ana de Jesus from the Beas community, but the headstrong Ana earned Teresa's wrath by taking too many nuns with her, against Teresa's orders. There was not enough room for them in the new foundation, so some of them had to be sent back. Teresa had learned from experience to take only a few sisters with her at first until the house was ready for a proper community.

John left early the following morning, and they were never to meet again. These two great souls will forever be linked, two of the greatest mystics and reformers of the Church. They were united in their burning love of God, but seemingly never seemed to really understand that the other was being led to the goal of union with God by different ways.

Onset of cancer

Teresa left for Burgos on 2nd January, a dreadful journey made in the depths of winter. She felt nauseous constantly, and suffered from a chronic sore throat - it turned out to be cancer - which made it difficult for her to eat. There was sleeting snow and rain the whole way, and at one point their wagon broke down as they were trying to ford a swollen river. Teresa was tipped into the icy water, so it was understandable that she complained bitterly to God. 'Teresa,' was the reply, 'that's how I treat my friends.' Teresa, never short of a riposte, replied, 'Yes, Lord, that's why you have so few!'

By the time the party arrived in Burgos, Teresa was spitting blood and went to bed. As usual, there were problems - the bishop had changed his mind about approving the foundation. Our Lord strengthened her,

'Now, Teresa, hold fast.' Gracián was one of the party, but he soon left - it was another final parting. Thankfully, Teresa did not live to see him captured and tortured by pirates, expelled from the Order, but finally admitted to the Calced.

Teresa stayed in Burgos to see the foundation established and restored after the house flooded. She was on her way to Avila for the Profession of Teresita, a young niece of hers, when she received an order to go to Alba de Tormes. The Duchess of Alba's daughter-in-law was about to give birth, and what better than to have a saint there to make sure that all would be well? It distressed Teresa deeply, but Fr Angelo, the vicar general insisted, so she had no choice but to obey. The Duchess this time had the courtesy to provide a carriage, but she had not thought to provide any food for them. At one dreadful inn the devoted Sr Ana of San Bartolomé could find only a few dried figs to give the sick nun, and at another a few onions. She recorded the distress she felt: 'When I saw that nothing could be found to buy, I could not look at the Saint without weeping, for judging by her face she seemed half dead. I can never describe the anguish I then felt. My heart seemed to be breaking, and I could only weep when I saw the plight she was in, for I saw her dying and could do nothing to help her.'

Last days

When they arrived at Alba they found the journey had been for nothing. The Duchess's daughter-in-law had already safely given birth. 'So they didn't need this old saint after all,' was Teresa's dry comment. The nuns, realising that Teresa really was dying, had prepared a bed with fresh sheets, and a clean habit for her, and Teresa went to bed earlier than she had ever done before.

Amazingly, she recovered enough to attend Mass daily, and recite the Divine Office. She had words with a rector from Salamanca who wanted the nuns to move into a new house. Teresa was opposed because it would be in a noisy area. When she could not be persuaded, Fray Agustín mentioned that he had already bought the house: - the deed was done. 'Is it?' Teresa replied. 'Anything but done, nor will it ever be.' The negotiations collapsed eight days after her death.

She made arrangements for elections, and reprimanded the outgoing Prioress for a laxity that the sisters had abused. On 28th September she collapsed, bleeding vaginally from cancer of the uterus, and took to her bed. She was in acute pain, and repeated often words from Psalm 51, 'a humble, contrite heart, O Lord, you will not spurn.' A perfume pervaded the whole house, and a sister in the kitchen found that even a salt cellar that Teresa had touched was scented. On 3rd October in the afternoon, Teresa asked Padre Antonio to bring her Communion, and while she waited she asked the assembled nuns for their pardon for the bad example she had given them.

When the Sacred Host was brought into the room her face became radiant, and she looked much younger. The impulse of her love almost lifted her from the bed, and she greeted her Lord in words of poignant love: 'O my Lord and my Spouse, now the hour has arrived for us to go forth from this exile, and my soul rejoices in oneness with You over what I have so much desired.' She expressed her gratitude for dying as a daughter of the Church.

The following day she remained motionless in prayer, her crucifix in her hands, in a deep peace and silence. Ana of San Bartolomé remained by her side all day, but when she went to get something to eat Teresa noticed she had disappeared. When Ana returned Teresa smiled at her and tenderly cradled her head in the little sister's arms. She remained like that until nine o'clock in the evening, surrounded by all the nuns, and her soul slipped peacefully away to the full vision of the Lord she loved so much.

Her face turned as white as alabaster; all signs of suffering and wrinkles of her sufferings smoothed away, and took on an extraordinary beauty. A strong perfume flowed from her body throughout the whole house.

Her great soul had died to this world, but she is truly alive, not only in heaven in the presence of God, but also in the exceptional spiritual legacy she has left us.